Tales Alive!

BIRD TALES
from
NEAR & FAR

DATE DUE			

DEMCO 38-296

BOOKS BY SUSAN MILORD

ADVENTURES IN ART
Arts & Crafts Experiences for 8- to 13-Year-Olds

Tales Alive!
BIRD TALES FROM NEAR & FAR
with Activities

HANDS AROUND THE WORLD
365 Creative Ways to Build Cultural Awareness &
Global Respect

THE KIDS' NATURE BOOK
365 Indoor/Outdoor Activities and Experiences

TALES ALIVE!
Ten Multicultural Folktales with Activities

TALES OF THE SHIMMERING SKY
Ten Global Folktales with Activities

Tales Alive!

BIRD TALES
from
NEAR & FAR

RETOLD BY SUSAN MILORD

PAINTINGS BY LINDA S. WINGERTER

WILLIAMSON PUBLISHING COMPANY
CHARLOTTE, VERMONT

For David, *rara avis*

This book would never have gotten off the ground were it not for the combined efforts of some very special people. Many thanks to both Jack and Susan Williamson, for their continued dedication to creating meaningful books for children; to Bill Jaspersohn, whose clarity of vision makes him an exceptional editor; to Joseph Lee, for designing a stunningly beautiful book; to Linda Wingerter, for the truly soaring artwork that graces the tales; and to Yvette Santiago Banek, for the wonderful, inviting activity illustrations.

LIBRARY OF CONGRESS CATALOGING-IN-PUBLICATION DATA

Milord, Susan.
Tales alive!: Bird tales from near & far/Susan Milord.
p.   cm.
Includes index.
Summary: Presents folktales and facts about birds from around the world.
Includes related handicraft, nature, science, and cooking activities.
ISBN: 1-885593-18-X
[1. Birds—Folklore. 2. Folklore. 3. Birds. 4. Amusements]
I. Title.
PZ8.1.M625 Tal   1998
[398.2]—dc21   97-39453
CIP
AC

Tales Alive!® is a registered trademark of Williamson Publishing Company

Paintings by **Linda S. Wingerter**
Activity illustrations by **Yvette Santiago Banek**
Design by **Joseph Lee Design, Inc.**
Printing by **Quebecor Printing, Inc.**
Printed in Canada

WILLIAMSON PUBLISHING COMPANY
P. O. Box 185
Charlotte, VT 05445
Telephone: 800-234-8791
10 9 8 7 6 5 4 3 2 1

Contents

Take Flight!

Have you ever heard the soulful cry of a mourning dove, or marveled at the effortless flight of a falcon? Perhaps you've watched a pair of robins making countless trips to a nest with food for their young, or even coaxed a chickadee to take a sunflower seed from your hand. If you have, you know what it's like to fall under the spell of birds. Birds are wonderful creatures in the true meaning of the word: they never fail to fill us with a sense of amazement and awe.

It may be their ability to fly that makes birds so intriguing, or the beauty of their melodies that draws us near. Certainly their willingness to feed and nest close to people endears them to our hearts. Of all the wild creatures, birds offer us the closest glimpse into their lives. No doubt this goes a long way to explaining our fascination with them.

No doubt, too, as long as people have been noticing birds, they've been telling stories about them. *Bird Tales from Near & Far* is a collection of six such stories, accounts that have been handed down from one generation to the next. These stories are among the best folk literature has to offer: Here are tales that seek to explain the mysteries of the natural world,

invite us into other cultures, even make us examine our own human foibles. Not surprisingly, the Ukrainians imagined the crow, a highly intelligent bird, as a powerful tsar ruling over a vast kingdom. The Iroquois used an owl—whose vanity proves to be his downfall—as an opportunity to point out how the same might prove true for humans.

But this book is more than a collection of stories. Each tale is followed by related activities, projects, and information about birds. For example, the Thai story "Mark My Words" features birds that speak the language of humans. The accompanying activities explore various aspects of real bird "talk"—the sounds we describe as calls and songs. You'll find hints for recording bird song on audio tape, and meet some of the birds named for the sounds they make. There's also a shadow puppet—complete with moving beak—for you to craft, plus the words and music to an Australian song about a bird with a most unusual call.

And so it is for the other stories in this collection. You'll venture into worlds where birds challenge mighty rulers, travel between heaven and earth, and bring great happiness to those around them. And after each tale, you'll find ample opportunity to get to know and understand our fine feathered friends better. In all, there are dozens of things for you to do and make, from constructing a nesting box for the birds in your neighborhood to stenciling a thunderbird design to whipping up a recipe for edible birds' nests!

So, let these fanciful tales of birds and their accompanying activities lift you off the ground. Take flight with *Bird Tales from Near & Far!*

About the Activities in this Book

The activities that follow each story serve to bring the tales to life as well as introduce you to some fascinating facts about birds. To fully enjoy the activities, keep in mind the following:

• Read all the way through a project before starting it. That way you'll know just what materials are needed and which steps (if any) may require an adult's help. Don't have enough time to complete a project in one sitting? No problem. Most projects have convenient stopping points, so you can leave your work and come back to it later.

• Be sure to get an adult's help when using tools you may be unfamiliar with, or if you're not old enough to use the tools on your own. Whenever a grown-up's help is required, you'll be reminded to ask for it in the project's instructions. Also, if you don't have everything a project calls for, an older person may be able to suggest alternative materials you can use.

• Have fun!

Imaginative tales about the origins of animals have been recounted by storytellers since the beginning of time. This Iroquois tale explains not only why the great horned owl looks the way it does, but also why it's never seen during the day.

Why Owl Hides During the Day

The first birds created by Everything-Maker were fine creatures, fine creatures indeed. They had beautiful brown feathers, strong wings, and beaks that were, well, just the right size. There was only one problem: Every single bird looked like this. Because they noticed that other living things were varied—some this color, some that, some thin, and some fat—the birds went to Everything-Maker to ask if they, too, could be different.

"None of the flowers are the same," Cardinal pointed out. "Violets are tiny with nodding purple faces, roses smell sweet, and the goldenrod is tall and yellow. Why must we all look alike?"

"No reason," said Everything-Maker. "Since you aren't happy the way you are, why don't you tell me how you'd like to look."

"Well, I, for one, wish to be red," said Cardinal.

"That's easy enough," replied Everything-Maker, tinting Cardinal's feathers the color of ripe cherries. "Next?"

Swan asked for white feathers and a long, arching neck. Nothing easier. Presto! Swan's neck twisted this way and that as she admired her snowy feathers. Egret liked Swan's new look so much she requested the same, only she wanted longer legs and a spear-like beak. Snap! Done. "Look at me! Look at me!" she exclaimed, parading before the other birds.

And so it went, as each bird stepped forward and asked Everything-Maker to give him feathers of a certain color, or a voice of a certain pitch, or feet that could wrap around the tiniest of branches, or beaks that were just so.

Throughout all of this, Owl was perched on a branch, waiting his turn. But the bird wasn't content to wait silently. He craned his neck to watch the goings-on and sneered at the other birds' choices. For instance, when Cedar Waxwing requested a dashing black mask, Owl let out a hoot. "Whoo! Whoo! Where do you think you're going? To a masked ball?" And when shy Hummingbird asked for shimmering green feathers and a ruby-red throat, Owl sneered, "A little flashy, don't you think?"

Now and then Everything-Maker shot Owl a look that would have silenced any other bird. But not Owl. He kept right on jabbering. Owl told Crossbill his twisted beak would never work properly, and he made fun of Chickadee's little black cap. When he saw the ruffled feathers on top of Phoebe's head, he laughed and jeered, then asked if she wanted to borrow a comb.

"Owl, that's enough," Everything-Maker said firmly. "If you don't have anything nice to say, then don't say anything at all."

"I can't help it," Owl whined. "I'm only pointing out what I see."

"Then turn around so that you're not watching. Either that or close your eyes."

But Owl refused to stop watching, and he continued to tease the other birds. "You are all such simpletons!" he scoffed. "Long beak here, spotted feathers there. Just wait till you see what I look like. I'm going to have a long neck like Swan's, red feathers like Cardinal's, broad wings and grasping claws like Eagle's, and a striped tail like Blue Jay's. I'll be the handsomest, the fastest...the most magnificent bird of all!"

That did it. Everything-Maker reached up and grabbed Owl off the branch. With one hand, he pushed the bird's head deep down into his body. Then holding the creature by both ears, he began to shake Owl so wildly that his eyes opened wide, as big and round as saucers.

"There," Everything-Maker said, setting the dazed and disheveled Owl back on his feet. "I hope you like the way you look. You don't have much of a neck, but at least now you won't be able to watch what you're not supposed to. Your ears are plenty big, too, so perhaps you'll listen when someone tells you what not to do. As for your eyes, they won't do you any good when the sun is shining. They're much better suited to the dark. Enjoy your nights, Owl. When you're awake, the rest of us will be fast asleep.

"Oh, and one last thing," Everything-Maker concluded. "Just in case you were thinking you'd at least get the feathers you wanted...Here!" With that, he smeared a handful of mud all over Owl's body.

Well, that put an end to Owl's mischief. The big bird flapped his broad wings and flew off to nap for the rest of the afternoon. That's what you'll find him doing most afternoons these days, if he's at all wise.

Iroquois

Feathered Facts

When is the best time to watch birds? Usually early morning and late afternoon. That's when many land birds are most active. Wait until dark if you hope to spot nocturnal birds such as owls.

Birds are naturally curious and will often come to investigate when they hear certain sounds. Try pishing—the term birders use to describe slowly blowing out air while saying "piiissshhh." Squeaking works well, too. Press your lips against the back of your hand and suck in your breath. By moving your hand, you can vary the sound.

You don't need a blind, of course, to observe birds. You don't even need to be outside. Just look out the windows of your house or apartment. Are there birds scurrying across your lawn? Nesting in nearby bushes? Roosting on fire escapes?

Hide and Seek

While it's true that most owls hide during the day (well, they're actually roosting, or resting), the majority of birds are plainly visible during the daylight hours. Because of this, no matter where you live, you are likely to see at least one kind of bird every day.

While watching birds can be as easy as looking up into the sky, if you would like to study birds more closely, you might want to conceal yourself behind a special hideout called a blind. Below are several ideas for simple blinds you can make yourself.

Flying Feathers

Native Americans have long used feathers for decoration as well as for ceremonial purposes. Eagle feathers are particularly revered.

Feathers also have many practical purposes, including uses in amusements and games. The cob flyer in this traditional Iroquois game certainly wouldn't fly as high without them.

To play the game, hit the cob from player to player using table-tennis paddles or badminton racquets. You can make the game more competitive by keeping score. Start with a score of 10; a player loses a point when he fails to hit the cob or return it to the other player. The player with the higher score wins.

For an even greater challenge, kick the cob back and forth using your feet. A similar game has been played in Asia for more than 2,000 years.

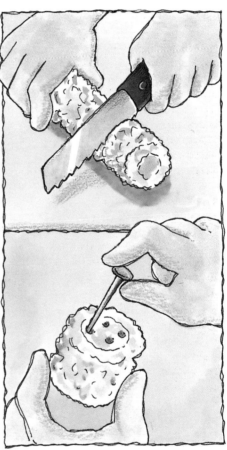

1 Have an adult help you cut a 1½-inch (4-cm) length of corncob with the saw or knife.

2 Using a nail or other sharp tool, poke four to six holes in the center of one flat side of the cob. Glue feathers in the holes. Let dry.

Feathered Facts

Feathers, and feathers alone, distinguish birds from other creatures. All birds have feathers, yet no other animal has them.

Beaks and More Beaks

Beaks are specially adapted to the types of food birds eat. Stout beaks can easily crack nuts and seeds. Long, narrow beaks are perfect for probing for nectar in flower blossoms, or for tiny animals in mud. Some fish-eating birds spear their dinner with their beak; others use their bill like a giant scoop.

Hawk

Long-billed Curlew

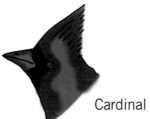

Cardinal

While most bird feet are used for perching, others are good for walking on soft sand, or scaling up and down trees. Some feet are designed like paddles, while others are made for grasping prey.

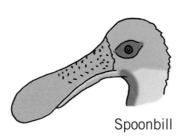

Spoonbill

Perching

Paddling

Grasping

Broad wings are best for soaring flight; the wings of fast-flying birds tend to be flat, narrow, and somewhat triangular in shape. Hummingbirds have swept-back wings that beat in a figure eight pattern, enabling them to hover in place.

Swift

Soaring

Hummingbird

Most birds are rather drab in color, providing them with all-important camouflage. The males of some species, however, are brightly colored.

Painted Bunting

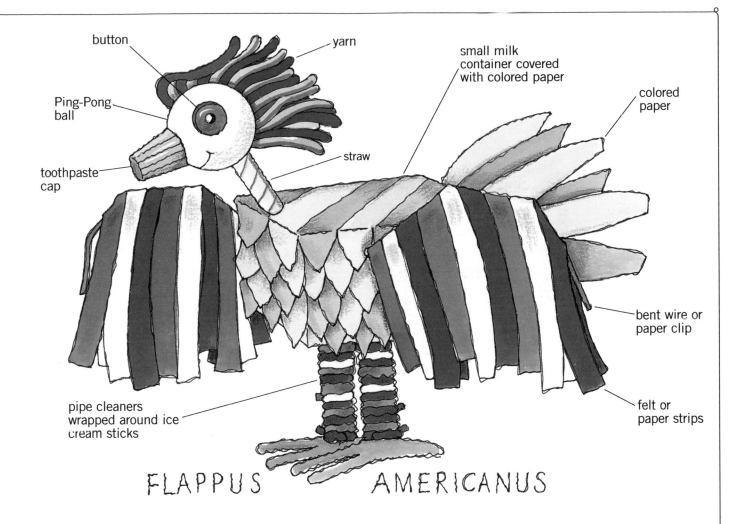

button

yarn

small milk
container covered
with colored paper

Ping-Pong
ball

colored
paper

toothpaste
cap

straw

bent wire or
paper clip

pipe cleaners
wrapped around ice
cream sticks

felt or
paper strips

FLAPPUS AMERICANUS

All the Better to...

Happily for bird-watchers, Everything-Maker gave the birds the beaks, feet, and feathers they asked for—all of which make it a lot easier to tell the different species apart!

Of course, birds don't look different for the benefit of bird-watchers. Each species is specially adapted to the environment in which it lives. As you can see on the previous page, a bird's size and shape, coloration, and type of beak

and feet say a lot about where and how it lives.

If you could design a bird, what would it look like? Using some everyday materials and your imagination, create a bird that might impress even Owl!

Invent and assemble a bird using various materials and hot glue. Make your bird free-standing, or attach a loop to hang it from a ceiling or doorway.

Up in the Air

YOU NEED
- 8½ by 11 inch (216 by 279 mm) paper
- Scissors
- Stapler

Birds are truly magnificent flying machines. Adjusting the feathers of their wings and tails, birds can swoop and swerve and maneuver in and out of tight spots with great precision.

You can get an idea just how birds control flight by making a paper glider with flaps. By adjusting the position of the flaps, you can make your glider turn one way or the other, even loop the loop.

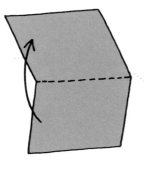

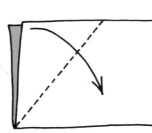

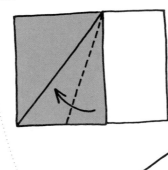

1 Fold the sheet of paper in half the short way. Fold the top left-hand corner down, then fold the right-hand edge up to meet the fold line. Turn the paper over and repeat. Return to the original position.

2 Flatten the paper, turn it over, and cut along the dotted line indicated. Refold the paper.

cut to this point

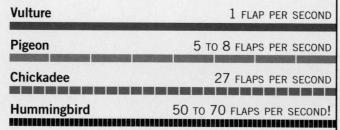

Faster! Faster!

All flying birds take off by flapping their wings, and many continue to move them up and down in a steady rhythm. Just how often does a bird flap its wings? It varies from species to species.

Try flapping your arms in time with a vulture. Can you flap as fast as a pigeon? Don't worry. No human being can flap as fast as a chickadee or hummingbird!

1 Second

Vulture	1 FLAP PER SECOND
Pigeon	5 TO 8 FLAPS PER SECOND
Chickadee	27 FLAPS PER SECOND
Hummingbird	50 TO 70 FLAPS PER SECOND!

Feathered Facts

Not all birds fly. Penguins don't (although they zip through water as fast as many birds do through the air). Neither do African ostriches nor the birds related to them. These include the South American rhea, Australian emu, and both the cassowary and kiwi of New Zealand.

3 Fold the top layer of the left-hand edge down, as shown. Fold over once again. Turn the paper over and repeat.

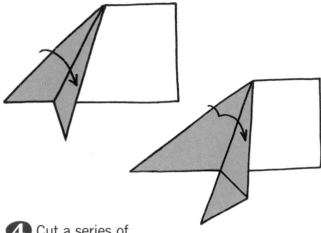

4 Cut a series of flaps along the unfolded edge.

5 Cut off the ends of the points near the angled folds. Open up the paper, overlapping the points as shown. Turn the paper over, then staple across the center crease. Bend the wings up slightly.

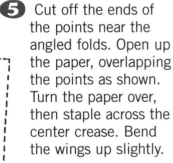

cut

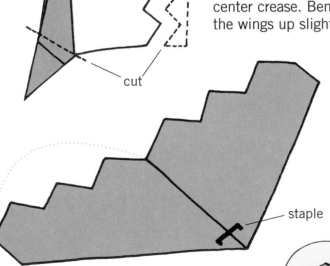

staple

underside view

To launch the glider, hold it at shoulder level, and gently give it a push at a downward angle. Adjust the flaps to change the direction of flight. Can you make the glider turn to the right? To the left? What about making it loop the loop? (Hint: Push all the flaps up, then toss it straight up into the air.)

Fabulous Feathers

A bird's body is covered by six types of feathers (some are found only on certain birds).

The feathers that cover the outer surface of a bird's body, its wings, and form its tail are called contour feathers. Contour feathers are stiff and strong.

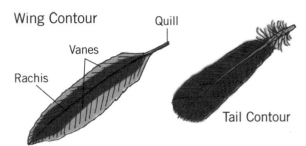

Wing Contour

Quill

Vanes

Rachis

Tail Contour

Semiplume feathers look like contour feathers, but their shafts are thinner and the vanes soft. Semiplumes help to cover a bird's body.

Semiplume

Filoplumes are hair-like feathers that grow in circles around some of a bird's contour feathers. They serve as receptors, "telling" a bird when its feathers need to be smoothed or adjusted in flight.

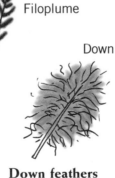

Filoplume

Down

Down feathers are small and fluffy, with very thin, short shafts. They provide wonderful insulation and are most numerous on ducks and other waterfowl.

Powder down feathers dissolve into a fine powder, and are found on birds such as pigeons, hawks, and herons. Short feathers called bristles grow around the beaks of birds such as flycatchers, and around the nostrils of woodpeckers.

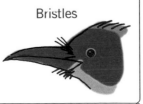

Bristles

Splish Splash

Bathing is an important part of keeping feathers in tip-top shape. Most birds bathe in water, but birds in arid, or dry, regions take dust baths. (Some birds, such as house sparrows, often follow a water bath with a dusting.)

Birds that spend most of their time flying, such as swallows, dip into water while they're on the wing. But most prefer wading into shallower water, and a shallow-water bath is something you can provide the birds in your backyard.

Below are several ideas for homemade birdbaths. Birds prefer firm footing, so if the bowl of your bath has a slick surface, add some sand to the bottom of it. Place your birdbath near a bush or tree where the birds can easily fly to safety to dry off.

Feathered Facts

Birds spend a lot of time preening, or smoothing, their feathers so that the barbules are interlocked. A bird uses its beak or its feet, or sometimes the help of another bird, when preening. Most birds also have a gland at the base of the tail that secretes oil. The birds use their beaks to squeeze the gland and spread the oil over their feathers to give them a protective waterproof coating.

Vanes

Barb

Lower umbilicus

Barb

Shaft or rachis

Barbule

Hooks

Search for feathers on the ground. If you find a contour feather, run your fingers along its length, from the feathery end toward the hard tip. Notice how the barbs, the parts of a feather branching off from the central shaft, separate. Now run your fingers in the opposite direction. With a few strokes, you should be able to smooth the feather to its original shape.

If you were to greatly magnify the feather, you could see that the barbs themselves are divided into many tiny branches called barbules. The barbules that angle toward the quill end have hooks along their length; those facing the feathery tip are smooth. When you smooth the feather in the right direction, the hooked barbules fasten onto the smooth ones, creating a flat, continuous surface.

Some of the world's most beautiful birds live in Southeast Asia. This tale from Thailand (formerly known as Siam) describes what happens when one of these, a lorikeet, or type of parrot, is captured and caged by a less-than-honest man.

Mark My Words

Long, long ago in a small village in old Siam, a man woke to find a lorikeet in his bedroom.

"Get out of here, you crazy bird!" said the man, waving his arms to shoo away the intruder.

"As you wish," the lorikeet answered and flew out of the window.

"Wait a minute!" exclaimed the man, leaping from his bed and running after the bird. "Did I hear what I thought I heard? You speak the language of man?"

"I do," replied the lorikeet.

"Well then," said the man quickly, "I take back what I said. You are a most amazing creature." Before the bird realized what was happening, the man clapped his hands around its body and tossed it into a bamboo cage.

Each market day, the man took the bird to the village square. There the townspeople crowded around its cage, totally captivated by the bird's lively chatter. While the lorikeet was not entirely happy being caged, one thing was certain—the living was easy. The villagers showered the talkative bird with the foods it loved best—nectar-laden blossoms and sugar water.

One night the lorikeet's keeper stole a water buffalo from his neighbor. The man was careful not to be seen leading the animal away, and somehow he managed to slaughter it without anyone being the wiser. What he didn't realize was that the lorikeet had witnessed everything.

When the neighbor found his buffalo missing the next morning, he asked the man if he had seen it. "I'm afraid not, neighbor," the man answered in his most earnest voice. "I wasn't feeling well last night. I went to bed early and didn't hear or see a thing until the sun woke me this morning."

"He's lying! That's not what happened," said the lorikeet.

The man was quick to contradict the lorikeet. "What a silly bird! The chatterbox was sound asleep in its cage before I even went to bed."

But the more the neighbor thought about it, the more he wondered which to believe: the man or the bird. He reported what he'd learned to the local magistrates. Everyone agreed: The lorikeet spoke the language of humans with full understanding. Very likely the creature knew exactly what had happened to the neighbor's buffalo. It was decided that the lorikeet's owner should be given a trial, and the bird would be called as a witness.

For days, the man could hardly sleep, so sure was he that the lorikeet's testimony would be enough to sentence him to jail. He considered getting rid of the bird, but knew that if it disappeared, the villagers would suspect he killed it to save his own skin. Then the man had a brilliant thought. The night before the trial was scheduled, he covered the lorikeet's cage with a large iron cooking pot. All night long, he splashed water on the pot so that the bird would think it was raining.

The next morning, both the man and the lorikeet stood before the

Mark My Words

village judge. A large crowd of people gathered to watch the trial. The judge said, "You are accused of stealing and killing your neighbor's buffalo. What do you have to say to this?"

Before the man could answer, the lorikeet screeched, "He stole it! He killed it! He ate it!"

"Your honor," said the man, "you aren't going to take a lorikeet's word over mine, are you?" He let out a laugh to show how absurd this was.

It struck some in the courtroom as funny, too. A few villagers openly smiled, while several others raised their eyebrows and shook their heads. But the judge said simply, "The bird has shown that it speaks our language well."

"So it has," replied the man. "But it tells such stories. I've learned not to trust what it says. Why, just ask this crazy bird what the weather was last night."

The lorikeet didn't wait to be asked. "What a rain that was!" squawked the bird. "It never let up, not for a minute. I heard it drumming on the roof all night long."

The villagers were stunned into silence.

"See what I mean?" the man said.

"You've proven your point," admitted the judge. "The bird is not a reliable witness." To the others in the courtroom he added, "As we have no way to prove that this man stole his neighbor's buffalo, we must let him go." And so the lorikeet's keeper walked away a free man.

And a much wiser one, too. Obviously, it was time to be rid of the lorikeet. Who knew what kind of trouble the bird might land him in next time. When he got home, the man opened the door of the cage. "Good riddance!" he said, as the bird flapped its way to freedom.

Some distance from the village, the lorikeet met a parrot. The parrot said, "I hear there is a fine village close by. A village where a bird might find plenty to eat."

"There is," replied the lorikeet. "You'll never go hungry if you don't mind living the rest of your life in a cage."

"Hmm. A cage, you say? Well, I think I could get used to that. Especially if it means never having to search for my own food again," said the parrot.

"To each his own," replied the lorikeet, shrugging. "But let me give you a friendly word of advice. As you are a handsome bird and as you speak their language, you will be of interest to humans. You will be well treated if you observe one rule."

"And what is that?" asked the parrot.

"Just remember that humans like to hear their own words echoed. You'll get along just fine if you repeat only those words that are spoken to you."

"That seems easy enough," said the parrot. "Well, I'll be on my way now. Thank you, my friend." And with that the parrot flew off in the direction of the village.

Sure enough, that afternoon the parrot caught the eye of a villager. "Say, aren't you a pretty bird," the villager remarked.

"Pretty bird, pretty bird," echoed the parrot, recalling the lorikeet's advice. From that day on, the parrot was careful to repeat only what was said to it. Just as parrots do to this day.

For a Song

The birds in "Mark My Words" were able to speak the language of humans. With a little practice, you should be able to speak one of the languages spoken by birds. Using only your hands, you can imitate the plaintive cry of the mourning dove, a bird whose name aptly describes its sad-sounding call.

1 Cup your hands tightly around a small pocket of air. It's important that there are no leaks. Press your thumbs together, bending the tops down as shown. Leave a small opening below the thumb joints.

2 Place your lips against your thumbs, taking care not to cover the opening below the joints. Slowly blow onto the thumb joints, holding your lips loosely and your tongue back. Adjust the position of your lips until you get a full, rich sound. By releasing your outer fingers, you can change the pitch.

Can you get any mourning doves to return your coo-ah, coo, coo, coo?

Extra! Extra!

Try making the sound of the loon with your cupped hands. Or invent your own calls. You and your friends can use these calls to signal each other, even when you're not within sight of one another.

Me, A Name I Call Myself

Some birds are named after the sounds they make. The phoebe gets its name from its call, a fuzzy fee-bee. Cat-like mewing is one of the sounds that—you guessed it!—the catbird makes. Below are some other birds that call out their names.

Black-capped Chickadee—chick-a-dee-dee-dee
Bobwhite—bob-WHITE or poor-bob-WHITE
Dickcissel—dick-dick-cissel
Killdeer—kill-DEEE
Whip-poor-will—whip-poor-will

Can you think of some other birds who are named after their calls? Check a field guide—or an audio recording—to help you add to this list.

Killdeer

Black-capped Chickadee

Feathered Facts

Ornithologists divide bird sounds into two broad categories—calls and songs.

CALLS ARE GENERALLY
- shorter in length
- a way for birds to advertise their location or to give warning
- thought to be innate (that is, birds are born knowing how to make them)

SONGS ARE GENERALLY
- longer in length
- sung by only certain birds (mostly the ones we call "songbirds")
- learned—usually from parents or others of the same species

Whip-poor-will

Feathered Facts

Both female and male birds call, but, with few exceptions, only males are singers. Males use song to both claim and defend territory as well as to advertise for mates.

Talk Show

Parrots are among the few birds known to mimic human speech. (Oddly enough, they do this only in captivity. In the wild, they don't imitate any sounds.) You can get a parrot to say almost anything—that is, if it's a parrot puppet!

The following is called a shadow puppet and was inspired by those used in Java, an island in Indonesia. Shadow plays are also popular throughout India, China, and Southeast Asia, including Thailand, where the lorikeet story takes place.

YOU NEED

- White poster board
- Scissors
- Paper fasteners
- Paint or markers
- Paint stirrer
- Long straight wire, such as florist's wire
- Masking tape

1 On a piece of poster board, draw the body, hooked top beak, and wing of a parrot. Cut out the three parts with scissors. Using the very tip of the scissors, punch small holes in the poster board where indicated. Be careful when using sharp scissors. If necessary, have an adult help you.

2 Paint the parrot. (Even though traditionally shadow puppets are silhouetted behind a cloth screen, the actual puppets are brightly decorated.) Let dry.

3 Fasten the beak and wing to the body with paper fasteners. Tape the paint stirrer to the back of the body. Tape the end of one wire to the back of the top beak; cover the other end of the wire with tape. Attach a wire to the wing in the same way.

Operate your puppet behind a backlit cloth (such as a sheet stretched between two chairs), or, if you would prefer its colors to be seen, from behind a table.

Feathered Facts

Some birds mimic other birds. The mockingbird is one such bird. Ornithologists have recorded mockingbirds imitating 30 different bird species, as well as other animals and various machines.

King of the Bush

Birds aren't the only animals that sing, of course. Here's a popular song from Australia you can sing. It's about the kookaburra, a type of king-fisher found on that continent, which has a wonderful laughing cry.

① Koo - ka - bur - ra sits in the old gum tree, _ Mer - ry, mer - ry

king of the bush is he_____ ③ Laugh, Koo - ka - bur - ra, laugh,

④ Koo - ka - bur - ra, Gay your life must be!_____

Kookaburra sits in the old gum tree,
Eating all the gum drops he can see.
Stop, Kookaburra,
Stop, Kookaburra,
Leave some there for me.

Kookaburra sits in the old gum tree,
Counting all the monkeys he can see.
Stop, Kookaburra,
Stop, Kookaburra,
That's no monk—that's me!

NOTE: This song is often sung as a round. Try singing it that way with your family or friends. The circled numbers indicate when additional voices should begin singing.

Madge, Madge, Madge, put-on-your-tea-kettle-ettle-ettle

Song Sparrow

Feathered Facts

To some people, certain bird calls sound like words and phrases spoken in English. Listen carefully to some of the calls and songs of the birds listed here. Is this what you hear?

American Goldfinch—potato-chips
American Robin—cheer-up, cheerily, cheer-up, cheerily
Ovenbird—teacher, teacher, teacher
Song Sparrow—Madge-Madge-Madge, put-on-your-tea-kettle-ettle-ettle
White-eyed Vireo—quick-give-me-the-rain-check!
White-throated Sparrow—sweet, sweet, sweet, Canada, Canada, Canada

For the Record

You can record some of the interesting bird calls and songs you hear in your backyard. All you need is an audio tape recorder with a microphone.

It is best to make outdoor recordings on calm days, when air movement won't interfere with the sounds you wish to capture. Early morning, when most singing takes place, is best. Here are some more tricks to make the most of your recording sessions:

- Make a cage out of pipe cleaners and bend it around the base of the microphone. Drape a piece of loosely-woven fabric over the wire cage. This will create a shield of still air around the microphone, reducing wind noise.

- Watch to see where the birds' song posts, or usual singing places, are. Fix the microphone to a tall stick or hang it from a branch so that it is as close to the birds as possible. The birds will fly off but will soon return and resume their singing.

- Set the microphone up near a bird feeder. Is the bird chatter different here than at a song post?

Feathered Facts

About half of the world's birds—nearly 4,000 species—are classified as songbirds.

Extra! Extra!

Check your local library or bookstore for recordings of bird songs. Use the tape to not only help you learn calls and songs, but also to play for the birds in your back-yard. How do the birds react when they hear their own calls? What do they do when they hear the screech of a raptor, or bird of prey?

Flower Power

The lorikeet in the story was fed nectar from plant blossoms. You may be familiar with one of this continent's nectar-sipping birds, the hummingbird.

There are nearly two dozen types of hummingbirds that summer in North America, and you can attract the ones that live in your region with some of their favorite flowers. While the birds are partial to the color red, they seek many blooms that are tubular in shape. Include some of the flowering plants below in your home landscape and you may be rewarded with regular visits from these winged jewels.

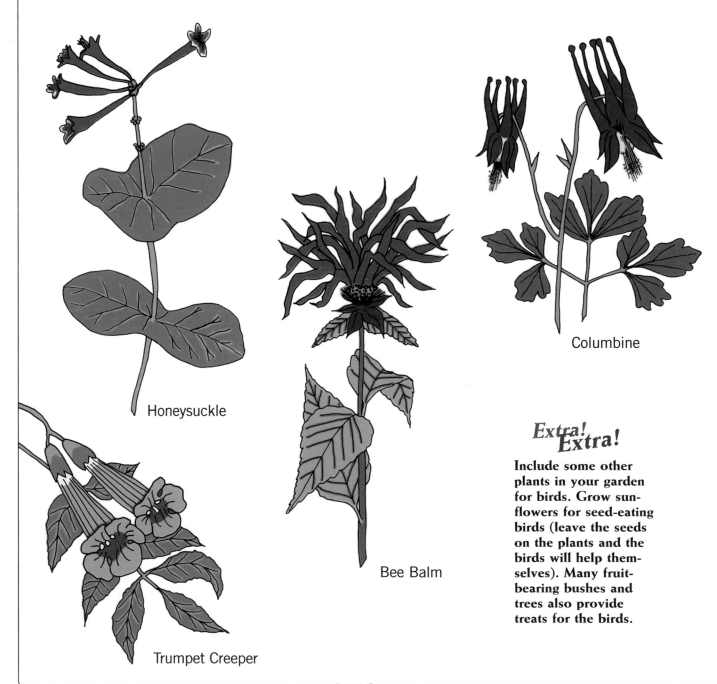

Honeysuckle

Columbine

Bee Balm

Trumpet Creeper

Extra! Extra!

Include some other plants in your garden for birds. Grow sunflowers for seed-eating birds (leave the seeds on the plants and the birds will help themselves). Many fruit-bearing bushes and trees also provide treats for the birds.

Humdinger!

Hummingbirds can also be enticed to dine near your home with homemade nectar. The birds are sure to spot this feeder, with its eye-catching designs!

1 Thoroughly wash and dry a small bottle or jar. Paint designs on the outside with red nail polish. Let dry completely.

2 Meanwhile, have an adult help you measure and mix 1/4 cup (50 g) sugar with 1/4 cup (60 ml) water in a small saucepan. Heat on the stove, stirring, until it comes to a boil. Remove from the stove, and stir in 3/4 cup (175 ml) cold water. Let the mixture cool completely.

3 Make a bow from red ribbon, and tie it around the jar's neck. Bend a piece of wire into a hanger. Hang the feeder from a branch, preferably near some red, yellow, or orange flowers. Fill the jar with the sugar syrup, then wait for the neighborhood hummingbirds to discover your gift to them.

Feathered Facts

The hummingbird is a marvel of movement. It can fly backward, straight up and down, as well as hover in place.

Hummingbirds also eat the insects and small spiders found in and around their favorite flowers.

NOTE: It is very important that you empty the jar and thoroughly clean it with hot, soapy water every two or three days. That's to prevent a harmful mold from growing in the sugar syrup that makes the birds sick.

There is also a concern that sugar syrup puts a strain on a hummingbird's liver. To minimize liver damage, once the birds have discovered your feeder, change the proportion of the syrup to 1 part sugar to 6 parts water.

King Solomon, who lived from about 970 to 930 B.C., was one of the kings of ancient Israel. He is best remembered for his celebrated wisdom. In this tale told throughout the Middle East, his judgment is challenged by a bird called a hoopoe.

The Palace of Beaks

Long, long ago, when time was measured by the trickle of sand, there ruled a wise and goodly king named Solomon.

It so happened that the birthday of King Solomon's wife was approaching, and the one gift—the only gift—the queen fancied was a palace made from the beaks of birds.

"And so you shall have one," said Solomon, who dearly loved his wife. He sent word that all the feathered creatures in his kingdom were to assemble before him one week hence.

When that day arrived, the air was filled with the noise of beating wings, punctuated by squawks and hoots and chirps. Birds of every kind had answered Solomon's call. There were cooing doves and long-legged storks, fearsome falcons and guinea fowl. There were terns and swallows, eagles and owls. Even the ostriches had made the long journey—on foot, as they cannot fly. But the king noted that among the birds there was not a single hoopoe.

"That's odd," King Solomon thought to himself. "I am surprised

Hoopoe is not here." The king had always felt great affection for the hoopoe, feelings which he thought the bird shared. But Solomon saw no reason to keep the other birds waiting. He would have to proceed without Hoopoe.

"I have asked you here today because the queen shall be celebrating her birthday soon," King Solomon told the feathered crowd. The birds began twittering excitedly. So, they were being invited to a party. How nice! Then one by one they noticed Solomon's finger on his lips. They ceased their chatter to listen. "For her birthday," Solomon went on, "the queen has asked for a palace made from the beaks of birds."

The birds fell silent, stunned by the king's words. Compared to the mighty lion or stately giraffe, they knew they were small and insignificant, but they hadn't expected this. Give up their beaks? What a dreadful

thought. How would they survive without beaks? On the other hand, if Solomon—wise and goodly Solomon—asked for their beaks, who were they to say no?

"You can place your beaks in a pile over there," King Solomon said, pointing. The birds began forming several lines, prepared to do the king's bidding.

At that very moment, Hoopoe arrived. The colorful bird dropped down in front of Solomon, who glared at the creature with undisguised impatience.

"And where have you been?" King Solomon asked.

"Flying hither and yon, my king," the hoopoe replied.

"Hmm," the king grunted. "Well, as I just finished telling the others, your beak is needed in order to build a palace for my wife."

Hoopoe listened and said nothing. He looked at the birds standing patiently in line, and then back at King Solomon. Finally he spoke. "I am sorry, Your Majesty, but I cannot give up my beak so readily."

"Oh? And why can't you?" The king cocked an eyebrow. "What makes you think you're any different from the other birds?"

"I am no different," Hoopoe began, "but in my travels I have learned many things. I ask you to listen to what I have to say."

"Very well," said King Solomon. "Proceed."

"I have a proposition: Here are three riddles. Answer all three correctly and I'll give up my beak without complaint," Hoopoe said. "But if you fail to answer even one of the riddles, you must allow all of us to keep our beaks."

The other birds were stunned by Hoopoe's boldness. How dare a mere bird challenge mighty Solomon! But the king admired the little bird's pluck. He also felt certain that he could answer the three riddles. "I agree to your bargain," he said simply.

37

The Palace of Beaks

"Very well," said Hoopoe, taking a deep breath. "Here is the first riddle. Who is it who was never born and shall never die?"

"Oh, that's an easy one," laughed King Solomon. "The Creator, of course. He who made all there is," he said, gesturing with his outstretched arms. "He who made the sky above us and the ground on which we stand. He who made the plants and the animals…and the birds." Solomon gazed thoughtfully at Hoopoe. And the birds, the monarch thought to himself.

"Here is the second riddle then," said Hoopoe, nervously clearing his throat. "Can you tell me what water neither rises from the ground nor falls from the sky?"

Solomon wasted no time in answering this one either. "That would be a tear," he said. "A tear that is shed in sadness." The king looked at the birds assembled before him. There was no mistaking the look of despair in their eyes. Sad thoughts began to fill Solomon's heart. When he reached up to touch his face his fingers were wet.

"Here then is the last riddle," said Hoopoe, his voice quavering. This was also the last chance to save the birds' beaks. "What is delicate enough to put food in a baby's mouth, yet strong enough to drill holes in wood?"

King Solomon's face creased in thought. He pulled on his beard. He looked skyward, and then at the sea of birds standing before him. His face broke out in a broad grin. "Why, that must be a beak, a bird's beak!" he said triumphantly.

But the king's satisfaction quickly dissolved into shame. He looked at the multitude of wondrous birds before him—birds in every size and shape imaginable, whose beaks were so essential to their survival—and he felt the weight of the world on his shoulders. Then he reached out and gently took Hoopoe in his hands, raising the bird high above his head.

Speaking loudly enough for all to hear, Solomon said, "I may have solved Hoopoe's three riddles, but he poses another question for which I

have no answer. And that is: Why should any of you give up your beaks? Your beaks are not mine to take. Hear this! There shall be no palace made from beaks!"

The great relief he saw in the birds' eyes was almost enough to make mighty Solomon weep. To the brave hoopoe in his hand he said, "It takes a wise man to know when he's been a fool. And what a fool I have been. My small friend, you have shown far greater wisdom than I. You are a king among birds!"

Asking Hoopoe to stay behind, Solomon addressed the others. "You may go now! Blessings upon you!" The grateful king then summoned his royal goldsmith and had him fashion a tiny crown for Hoopoe, which he carefully placed on the bird's head.

Hoopoe proudly wears the crown to this day, where it serves as a reminder that true wisdom can be found in even the smallest among us.

Birdbrain Teasers

King Solomon was not easily stumped by Hoopoe's three riddles, but you may have to think twice before coming up with the answers to the following bird-related puzzlers.

The following clever example is from Iran. Can you guess what is being described?

> There is a pair of doves. In their flight, they reach the skies, but they never leave their nest.

Give up? The answer is eyes. You have two eyes (a pair), and even when they look up (reach the skies) they are still in your head (nest).

Feathered Facts

Just how smart are birds? Much smarter than most people give them credit. While instinct plays an important role in bird behavior (don't forget, we humans are also guided by instincts), studies have shown that birds regularly react to situations in ways that appear to require thought.

The next rhyming riddle describes one of the wondrous creations of birds. Any idea what it is?

In marble walls as white as milk,
Lined with skin as soft as silk,
Within a fountain crystal clear,
A golden apple doth appear.
No doors there are to this stronghold,
Yet thieves break in and steal the gold.

If you said an egg, you're absolutely right. The last example is a math puzzler. On your marks, get set, start counting!

A duck before two ducks,
A duck between two ducks,
A duck behind two ducks.
How many ducks?

Not as many as you might think. There are only three ducks. Sneaky, huh? What other riddles or jokes do you know that feature birds?

Twist and Shout

Some devilish tongue-twisters are about birds, too. How fast can you say:

A bitter biting bittern bit a better biting bittern,
And the better biting bittern bit the bitter biter back;
Said the bitter biting bittern to the better biting bittern,
"I'm a bitter biting bittern bitten back!"

Come and Get It!

Feeding birds is one of the most popular ways of attracting them to backyards, especially in regions that get cold during the winter months. Birds use up a lot of calories keeping warm, and extra seed and suet can make a big difference to the species that overwinter in those areas.

The simpler the better is generally true when it comes to feeding birds. Fill birdfeeders with sunflower seeds—most birds love them. Toss a handful of seeds (with a little cracked corn, if you like) on the ground for those species that are ground-feeders.

Many birds also enjoy suet. Most supermarkets sell chunks of suet or suet balls (often bagged and ready to hang outdoors). You can also rig your own hanging suet feeders.

Feathered Facts

The birds in "The Palace of Beaks" were absolutely right: Without their beaks, they couldn't survive. Birds not only use their beaks to eat, they also use them like we use our hands, for doing everything from constructing nests to smoothing their feathers.

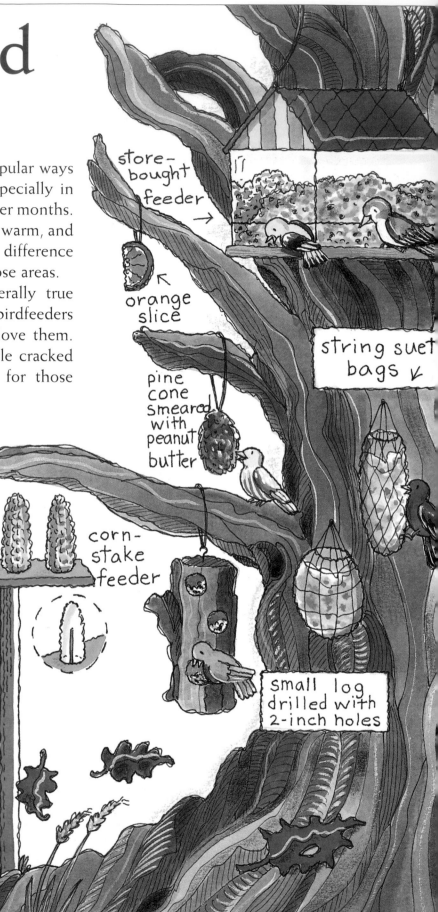

store-bought feeder →

← orange slice

pine cone smeared with peanut butter

corn-stake feeder

string suet bags ↓

small log drilled with 2-inch holes

coffee-can feeder

milk-carton feeder

Milk

evergreen or vine wreath with corn, cones, fruit slices, nuts, etc.

peanuts

store-bought feeder

Like a Bird

If your parents have ever accused you of eating like a bird, they probably meant you didn't eat very much. The truth is, most birds regularly eat one-quarter to one-half their weight in food each day!

To give you an idea how much food you'd need to consume daily if you were a bird, divide your weight by two and pile that amount of food on a bathroom scale. Bet your parents are glad you don't *really* eat like a bird!

Feathered Facts

In preparation for long migration flights, birds eat huge amounts of food. Some birds increase their weight by as much as 50 percent before they migrate.

See page 32 for garden plants you can grow to attract birds.

Robins and Bluebirds and Larks, Oh My!

Pileated Woodpecker seen on my birthday pecking on the tree near my bedroom

Feathered Facts

A bird-watcher is anyone who takes an interest in birds. Many bird-watchers provide food and nesting boxes for backyard birds.

The term birder is used for someone who is a more serious bird-watcher. Birders often travel distances in search of different species.

An ornithologist is a trained professional who studies birds and their behavior.

Here in North America, you aren't likely to come across any hoopoes except in zoos, but with nearly 700 different bird species to choose from (out of some 8,700 worldwide), there are plenty of others for you to get to know.

Bird-watching is the second most popular leisure time activity in this country (after gardening), and some birders have turned it into a sport of sorts. They keep what is called a life list, a personal record of birds sighted, noting where and when each was spotted.

You can compile your own life list. Start with the birds in your backyard. What bird is at the top of your list?

The Birds that Flock Together...

You know, of course, that birds gather in flocks (just as cows congregate in herds and fish swim in schools). But did you know there are special words to describe groups of particular birds?

A group of geese is properly called a gaggle, while a gathering of flamingoes is known as a stand. (Isn't that a perfect name for such long-legged birds?) Then there's a congress of crows, a paddling of ducks, and an exaltation of larks. Believe it or not, these are all real terms that were once in common usage.

Make up your own names to describe groups of birds. What outrageous—yet oddly appropriate—names can you come up with for woodpeckers or finches or herons or quail?

Crowning Achievement

"The Palace of Beaks" is a tale with a message: Even people with great intelligence and understanding sometimes make errors in judgment, while ordinary folk—or birds, as is the case in the story—are just as capable of acting wisely. But the story also serves to explain how the hoopoe came to have a crown-like crest. (The hoopoe's crest usually lies flat against its head, but when it's fanned, it looks just like a crown.)

Here's a play crown you can make, inspired by the beauty of birds.

1 Use the measuring tape to find the circumference of your head above your ears. Use that measurement to cut a strip of poster board a few inches longer by about 6 inches (15 cm) in height. Snip a series of points along one long edge of the strip.

2 Cut feather or bird shapes from extra poster board. Glue them directly to the strip, or suspend them above it with short pieces of wire taped to their backs. Decorate the strip and cutouts however you like.

3 Form the strip into a circle that fits comfortably on your head. Secure with glue.

YOU NEED

- Measuring tape
- Poster board
- Scissors
- Assorted papers, paints, and markers, buttons, sequins, and glitter, purchased feathers
- Glue

Feathered Facts

Many Native American peoples make crown-like headdresses from feathers. These are worn on special occasions and as part of ceremonial costumes.

Blackfeet Headdress

Can you think of any other birds with prominent crests? How about the cardinal, or the cedar waxwing? The roadrunner has a bushy crest, while the wood duck has a sleek green crest that almost looks like a helmet.

No Bones About It

In another version of this tale, King Solomon's wife asks her husband for a palace made from the bones of eagles. Bird bones are quite different from the bones of mammals. Because birds must be as light as possible in order to get off the ground and sustain flight, many of a bird's bones are actually hollow.

The best flyers have the greatest number of hollow bones, but even most of the bones of other birds have a unique structure. Save some bones from a chicken dinner, and carefully saw them in half. Be careful when cutting. Have an adult help you. Do you see the network of struts that strengthen the bone but keep it as light as possible?

Feathered Facts

To further save weight, some bones in a bird's body are fused, or joined together.

For more on bird flight, see page 16.

Diving Range

Not all birds have hollow bones. Birds that dive into water have relatively solid bones. You can see why solid bones would be better for diving with a simple experiment.

Using only one finger, push down on a tennis ball floating in a basin of water. Now do the same thing with a baseball. Which is easier to dunk?

Just as the heavier baseball is easier to push down into the water, so, too, the solid bones of loons and auklets make it easier for those birds to dive beneath the surface of the water.

Wish Upon a Bone

The wishbone, properly called the furcula, is unique to birds. It is one of the bones in a bird's skeleton that is fused—in this case, it's two collar bones united as one.

Break a wishbone as a way of seeing if a wish will come true.

Check a chicken carcass for the wishbone (it's located in the upper breast area). Clean it thoroughly and let it dry for several days. Find a partner, then each of you hook a pinkie around one end of the wishbone, make your wishes, and pull. Whoever is left holding the larger piece gets his wish. (You wish.)

Feathered Facts

Where did the custom of breaking wishbones originate? Possibly in Italy, when the Etruscans ruled that region (around 500 B.C.). At that time, wishbones were used to divine the future. The Romans adopted the practice, later taking it with them to the British Isles. Over fifteen hundred years later, it made its way to North America with the first colonists.

*This Ukrainian tale features a plot element found in many
European tales: Three siblings (in this case, brothers) try to solve a problem,
but only the youngest—the kindest—succeeds.*

The Farmer and the Tsar of the Crows

I cannot say when it happened, nor exactly where, but once upon a time there lived a poor farmer, his wife, and their three sons.

One spring day, the man and his youngest son were plowing a field when a great shadow fell across them. The two looked up to see an enormous crow, its ebony wings as broad as a house, circling above them.

"Tell me, old man," said the crow, gliding to the ground beside the frightened farmer. "Which shall it be? Your oxen or your son?"

"Whaa-at do you mean?" the farmer stammered.

"My little ones are hungry. I must feed them," the crow said. "Which shall it be? Your oxen or your son?"

What was the farmer to do? He couldn't possibly give up the oxen. They were his only animals, and without them he couldn't plow the fields

The Farmer and the Tsar of the Crows

nor harvest the grain on which he and his family depended. But surrender his son? Never! "You can't have either one of them!" he said defiantly. "Take me! Take me instead!"

"Phut," hissed the crow. "You won't do. You're too old and your flesh stinks of tobacco."

The farmer pleaded with the giant bird, but to no avail. Finally, he offered the bird his oxen.

"A wise choice," the crow said, flexing its powerful claws. "I'll take them. But not without paying. Send one of your sons to my palace. He'll find ample compensation waiting for him there."

"Your palace? I wouldn't know where that is," the farmer said.

"East of the morning star," the giant crow said simply. "Your son can ask directions along the way. Just have him mention my name, Tsar of the Crows." With that the enormous bird plucked the two oxen from the field as easily as if they'd been fallen apples. With a few flaps of his huge wings, he disappeared from view.

The farmer's wife began to sob when she heard what had happened to the oxen. "How will we ever survive?" she cried. "You haven't finished plowing the field, much less sown it with seed. Now there'll be no crop, and without a crop we'll have no bread."

The eldest son tried to comfort her. "Don't fret, Mother. I shall go to the palace of the Tsar of the Crows. With the money he gives me, we'll buy two more oxen, and all will be well."

Early the next morning, the boy's mother packed him a flatbread and an onion in a small shoulder bag. Waving good-bye to his family, the lad set out in the direction of the morning star.

The eldest son walked up hills and down hills, through fields and across streams, until he found himself in a dense forest. Stopping by a brook to quench his thirst, he decided to eat a little of his flatbread. He had just broken off a piece when a crow with a broken wing hopped up beside him.

"Good day," said the crow.

"Good day to you," replied the eldest son.

The crow hopped a little closer, cocking its head to stare at the flatbread. "I'm rather hungry," it said. "Might you share a bit of your meal with a lame bird?"

"I'm sorry, but I haven't enough to spare," the lad said. "I have a long journey ahead of me, and I'll need every bit of what I have."

"Where are you going?" the crow asked.

"To the palace of the Tsar of the Crows," the lad replied.

"Why, I'm headed there myself." the crow said. "But, with my broken wing, it's not easy…Let me perch on your shoulder, and I'll show you the way."

"I'm already tired," the boy said, annoyed by the bird's persistence. "I couldn't possibly carry you."

At this, the crow let out a piercing caw and flapped its wings and flew away.

"What cheek!" the eldest son exclaimed. "That bird could fly with no problem. And to think that I almost fell for its trick." He finished his meal and set off again in search of the palace of the Tsar of the Crows. But the lad took a wrong turn here and a false turn there, and couldn't find his way out of the forest.

The farmer and his wife waited a long time for their eldest son to return, but the days passed and still the lad did not appear. Their middle son begged to go and search for him. "Please, let me look for my brother. Even if I don't find him, perhaps I'll find the palace of the Tsar of the Crows. Then, at least, I can get what that thieving bird owes us."

The farmer and his wife reluctantly agreed, and the next morning the middle son set off, carrying a flatbread and onion in his bag. He tramped up hills and down hills, through fields and across streams, until he found himself in a dense forest. Of course, it was the same forest his older brother had gotten lost in, and when the middle son sat down to drink at the brook and to nibble at his flatbread, who should appear but a lame crow, begging for a bit of bread.

The boy had no more patience for the crow than his older brother had. "Feed you? It's not my job to feed you. Why don't you ask the Tsar of the Crows to feed you?"

"I would if I could make it to his palace. If you let me perch on your shoulder, I'll show you the way."

"Get a ride from someone else," the middle son snarled. At this, the crow took to the air and flew off.

"Look at that," muttered the middle son, watching the crow disappear from view. "That bird could fly with no problem. And to think that I almost fell for its trick." The middle son finished his meal and set off once again in search of the palace of the Tsar of the Crows. But he took a wrong turn here and a false turn there, and soon found himself as lost as his older brother.

The farmer and his wife were beside themselves with grief when the middle son did not return. They felt sure they would never see either of the boys again. Finally, the youngest son announced he would look for them.

"What good will that do?" the boy's mother asked, wiping her eyes. "Your two brothers were capable lads, and look what happened to them. You're the only one left. We can scarcely afford to lose you, too."

"Well, if I don't return, there'll be one less mouth to feed," the boy said in reply. And so he left home the next morning, carrying a flatbread and an onion in a bag, just as his two older brothers had done before him.

The youngest son skipped up hills and down hills, through fields and across streams, until he found himself in a dense forest. By now you've guessed it was the same forest his two brothers had gotten lost in. Just as the other two had done, the youngest son sat down to drink at the brook and to nibble at his flatbread. And just as happened twice before, a lame crow came hopping into the clearing.

"What I'd do for a bit of your bread," the crow sighed.

"Why, you needn't do anything for it," replied the lad, breaking off a piece and giving it to the crow. "There's enough for both of us, I'm sure."

"And may I have a bit of your onion as well?" the crow asked.

"But of course," the lad said.

The crow thanked the lad, then asked where he was headed.

"I'm on my way to the palace of the Tsar of the Crows," he told the bird. "I fear my two brothers are being held prisoner there."

Bird Tales from Near & Far

"If you let me perch on your shoulder, I'll show you the way," offered the crow.

"I'd be much obliged," the lad said earnestly.

The two traveled for three whole days and three whole nights. Just as the youngest son was thinking that he couldn't possibly walk another step, he noticed a bright light in the distance. The glow was coming from a clearing in the forest. As he cautiously made his approach, the lad could see that this was no ordinary clearing. Everything in it, from the grass and the leaves on the trees to the pebbles in the babbling brook, was made of silver. And there in the very center stood a glittering silver palace, guarded by crows.

The youngest son's guide said, "Here you are then—the palace of the Tsar of the Crows, and where we part company. Just one last word of advice: When the Tsar asks you what you want in exchange for the oxen, tell him you want nothing more than what he puts under his pillow each night."

"I would never have made it this far without your help," said the youngest son. "I'll do as you suggest. But will I ever find my brothers?"

"When the time comes," was all the bird would say. And off he flew.

The Tsar of the Crows stared, surprised, when the youngest son was brought before him. "So, you found your way here," he said. "I owe you for two oxen, and I always keep my word. Spend a few days with me in my palace. At the end of that time, you may choose any one thing you like as payment."

The youngest son spent three days in the palace, praying he would find his brothers, whom he had decided to take as his reward if he found them. But there was no trace of his two siblings, and when the day came for him to select his payment, he remembered the lame crow's advice. He told the Tsar, "Your home is filled with many wonders and riches. But all

I'd really like is what you place under your pillow each night."

"This is an outrage!" the mighty Crow screeched. "What do you know about what I keep beneath my pillow?"

When the youngest son refused to say, the Tsar was certain the crows who had shown the boy around the palace were responsible, and ordered them beheaded. This greatly frightened the youngest son, but he stood his ground. The Tsar of the Crows had promised him any one thing of his choosing, and what he wanted was what the Tsar kept under his pillow.

"Take it then!" spat the giant crow, finally giving in and handing the boy a tiny coffee-grinder. "Now get out of my sight, before I change my mind and have you beheaded!"

The youngest son took the grinder and fled from the palace, running for all he was worth. Only when his tired legs could carry him no farther did he sit down to rest. He was weak with hunger and cursed himself for not asking the Tsar for something useful, such as a basketful of food or some means of returning to his father's farm.

He looked down at the grinder in his hand and said aloud, "Oh, how I wish I were at home, sitting down to a grand meal with my mother, my father, and my two brothers." Absentmindedly, the boy turned the grinder's tiny handle.

That same moment, the lad found himself seated at his family's table, staring at a dozen platters piled high with food. And there sitting next to him were his parents and his two brothers! Such rejoicing you never heard!

And so the poor farmer, his wife, and their three sons lived happily ever after, and not so poorly anymore, either. For any time they needed something, they simply turned the handle of the grinder and their wishes would come true.

You may wonder how I come to know all this. That's no secret: The lame crow told me.

Nest, Sweet Nest

Real crows don't live in palaces, of course, or in shelters of any kind. They simply roost in trees. Only when it's time to raise a family do crows construct nests high in tree branches—soft cups designed to hold eggs and, later, hatched chicks.

Nest-making birds use an amazing array of materials to construct homes for their young. You can offer the birds in your backyard some soft nest-making ingredients. Just collect any of the items below, and put them where the birds can easily find them.

- Dried grass and moss
- Hair, from humans and pets
- Short pieces of string, yarn, dental floss

- Stuffing from old furniture
- Cotton balls
- Wood shavings
- Cellophane "grass" from Easter baskets

Feathered Facts

Most birds construct new nests each spring, so you can keep any you find in late autumn. Because a nest may contain hidden insects, place it in a sealed plastic bag with a few mothballs for a week or so.

Straw Into Gold

Did you know that birds' nests even find their way onto dinner tables? In China, a soup made from the nests of swallows that live in Malaysia is considered a real delicacy. Reported to possess the power to restore youth, the nests are actually quite nutritious.

You can make a dish inspired by birds' nests. Be sure to have an adult help you when cooking at the stove, as oil for deep-frying is very hot.

1 Peel the potatoes and coarsely grate them. Squeeze as much liquid from the them as you can; set aside.

2 Ask an adult to heat several inches of oil in a heavy saucepan until very hot. (Do not do this yourself, please.) Pack the bottom of the strainer with a handful of grated potato, forming a nest shape. Sprinkle with salt and pepper.

3 Carefully lower the strainer into the hot oil, and cook for 3 to 4 minutes, or until the bottom of the nest turns golden brown. With a heatproof utensil, carefully flip the nest over in the strainer and cook for an additional 2 to 3 minutes. Drain the nest on paper towels until cool enough to eat.

Serve the nests as a side dish, or fill them with other foods. Something made with eggs might be appropriate!

Feathered Facts

Once you see birds making nests, it won't be long before they start their families. (Some birds have just one brood a year; others have more.) Eggs will be laid, they will be kept warm until they hatch, and then the real work begins—feeding those hungry babies!

Watch to see how often the parents bring food for their young. Can you see how the babies are fed?

Box Number

Birds that raise their young in tree cavities are often happy to use man-made substitutes. The following nesting box, or birdhouse, is one that several different small birds find suitable. The front is designed to open, so that you can clean the box at the end of the season.

While the basic design appeals to a range of small birds, you can adjust the size of the entrance hole to make the box more attractive to particular species (and to discourage certain other birds from nesting in it). Where you place the birdhouse will also influence who uses it. Check the accompanying chart for specifics.

Feathered Facts

The best time to put up new birdhouses is in autumn. This not only gives their unpainted wood time to age, but the houses will be in place when the first birds return in spring.

Do you have any dead or dying trees on your property? If they don't pose any danger, leave them. Cavity-nesting birds will happily excavate their own homes in the soft wood.

1 Measure and mark the cutting lines on the two boards, as shown in the diagram. Be sure to also mark the locations of the various holes.

2 Cut out the pieces with the saw. Drill the entrance hole with the 1½" bit. Drill the hanging hole and the ventilation holes with the ¼" bit.

3 On the back of the front piece, scratch some horizontal lines beneath the entrance hole. These are footholds for the young birds, making it easier for them to climb out of the box when they are ready to leave the nest.

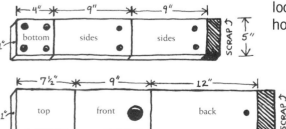

4 Assemble the box, as shown. Note that one side is not nailed, to allow it to swing open. Screw in the bent-screw fastener to close.

If you like, you can paint the exterior of the birdhouse. Be sure to choose a paint that can stand up to the weather. Ask your parents for any leftover exterior house paint or stain, remembering to prime the wood first to help the paint last longer.

Here are some of the cavity-nesting birds that you may entice to use your nesting box.

SPECIES	SIZE OF HOLE	HEIGHT FROM GROUND	PREFERRED HABITAT
House wren	1–1 1/4" (2.5 to 3.25 cm)	4–10 ft (1.25 to 3.5 m)	Edge of woods; backyards
Tree swallow	1 1/2" (4 cm)	4–15 ft (1.25 to 5 m)	Open areas, such as fields
Chickadee	1 1/8" (3 cm)	4–15 ft (1.25 to 5 m)	Edge of woods
Carolina wren	1 1/2" (4 cm)	5–10 ft (1.75 to 3.5 m)	Edge of woods; backyards
Bluebird	1 1/2" (4 cm)	3–6 ft (1 to 2 m)	Open areas, such as fields
Downy woodpecker	1 1/4" (3.25 cm)	5–15 ft (1.75 to 3 m)	Edge of woods
Titmouse	1 1/4" (3.25 cm)	5–15 ft (1.75 to 3 m)	Edge of woods
Nuthatches	1 1/4" (3.25 cm)	12–20 ft (4 to 7 m)	Edge of woods

Eggs-traordinary!

The Ukrainians have been decorating eggs for centuries, and their pysanky, or wax-resist eggs, are among the most beautiful in the world. The decorative symbols and colors have special meanings, many of which are meant to bring the egg's owner good luck.

The following scratched eggs, which are much simpler to make, are a specialty of neighboring Lithuania.

YOU NEED

- Raw egg, at room temperature
- White vinegar
- Cold-water egg dye
- Craft knife or other sharp tool
- Needle

1 Clean the egg in a solution of one part white vinegar to four parts water. Prepare the dye according to package directions, then fill a drinking glass with enough to cover an egg. Place the egg in the dye bath, and leave until it is the desired shade. Remove, rinse, and let dry.

2 Using the Ukrainian designs below, or your own, lightly sketch designs on the egg in pencil. Scratch over the lines with a craft knife, doing short sections and going over them, as needed, before moving on.

Bird

Feathered Facts

Many cultures around the world have long regarded eggs as a symbol of renewal and rebirth. The first people to exchange decorated eggs were the ancient Persians.

Some Traditional Pysanky Symbols

Sun

Triangle

Sun

Triangle

Sun

Plant

Sun

62

3 Poke a small hole in one end of the egg with a sharp needle; make a slightly larger hole at the other end. Placing your mouth over the smaller hole, blow the contents of the egg into a small bowl. (Refrigerate the egg content if it won't be used in cooking right away.) Wash out the shell with running water, then set aside until dry.

Roll Model

While most eggs are indeed "egg-shaped," there's plenty of variation in shape (not to mention size and coloration). Some owls lay round eggs; the eggs of the nighthawk are long and narrow. Seabirds that nest on bare rock lay eggs that come to a point at one end. A pointy egg rolls in a tight circle, and so is less likely to tumble off a cliff.

You can see just how this works. Give a chicken egg a gentle push and watch what happens. (Just in case, be ready to catch it!)

Feathered Facts

Birds with open nests tend to lay speckled or spotted eggs which blend in with their surroundings. Birds that lay eggs in cavities often lay white eggs, since there is no need for camouflage.

*Many cultures believed special messengers served as go-betweens between heaven
and earth. Not surprisingly, many of these messengers were birds.
(Luckily, not all were as absentminded as the one in this Galla tale from Ethiopia!)*

The Messenger Bird

hen The Maker created the people, he didn't know that a
lifetime spent under the searing sun would bake a man's skin
until it dried and cracked. He didn't know that a woman's
back would stoop from years of carrying babies and from
digging and hoeing the rocky soil.

How could The Maker know? The Maker never grew old. He was
always the same. But from his perch in the sky, he could see how the people started life as glistening, smooth-skinned babies, and how they ended
their days with little more than parched skin hanging from tired bones.

The Maker called Holawaka the Messenger Bird to his side.

"I want you to deliver an important message for me," he told
Holawaka. "Are you listening?"

"I am listening," said Holawaka.

"Go to the Galla people. Tell them that when their skins start to wrin-
kle and sag they can slip out of them and find fresh, new skins underneath."

"Oh!" The Maker's messenger said. "New skins for old ones. That's a good idea." But hardly necessary if the Galla were birds, he thought to himself. We birds replace our old feathers with new ones all the time. "But which ones are the Galla?" he wanted to know.

"You are a forgetful bird," The Maker said. "The Galla are the tall, black ones."

"Oh! Now I remember," said Holawaka. "Is that all then?"

"That's all for now," replied The Maker.

Holawaka flew down to earth to deliver the message to the Galla people. Of course he'd taken messages to the Galla before, but he really couldn't remember them being tall and black. Oh, well. He'd find out

where they were. "I'm sure I'll know them when I see them," he sighed.

The first creature the Messenger Bird came to was not tall and black. It was round and squat and appeared to have neither legs nor a head. "Hello!" Holawaka said brightly. "I have a message for the Galla."

The bird was startled when five scaly extremities shot out from all sides of the silent form. "I am not the Galla," said the sleepy turtle, some-what crossly, before its four legs and neck disappeared from view once again.

"So you're not," said Holawaka. "Sorry."

Holawaka flew on until he met a creature snipping short grass with its teeth. The creature was tall and black...and white. "Tall and black and white?" the bird wondered aloud.

"That's me," said the zebra.

"I have a message for the Galla," Holawaka said.

"That's not me," the zebra replied, returning to her grazing.

Holawaka flew on until he came upon another creature. This one was all black. It was long and black. Long and black is not much different than tall and black, Holawaka thought. "I have a message for the Galla," he announced.

"Oh?" said the long, black creature, a snake. "And just what is that message?"

"Oh, just something about staying young," replied Holawaka.

Well! This was something of great interest to the snake. But he knew Holawaka would never share the secret with him. It was meant for the Galla—Holawaka had said so. Still, the snake wondered if he might get the bird to volunteer the information...without realizing it. "That sounds like it would take a lot of work," the snake said matter-of-factly.

"Not at all," answered Holawaka. "Unless you call shedding your old skin for a new one a lot of work."

So that was it. "You mean like this?" asked the snake, slithering his way out of his skin.

"Just like that," said Holawaka, completely forgetting himself. "To be honest, I think the way we birds do it is much easier, much less of an inconvenience. We just drop the worn feathers and grow new ones in their place. Did you know we can even fly while we are molting our feathers?

But I guess this way will work, too. Say, let's see what you look like now."

But when Holawaka looked down all he saw was the long, transparent casing of a snake coiled on the ground. The bird had been talking to an empty skin. While he'd been jabbering on about this and that, the wily reptile had sidled out of sight.

Thanks to foolish Holawaka, snakes acquired the secret of staying young. And no thanks to him, the Galla people continue to grow old and stiff and eventually die, just like they always had and always will.

As for the Messenger Bird himself, The Maker was so annoyed that he had given the message to the snake instead of the Galla that he banished the bird from the Sky Kingdom. Holawaka has lived on earth ever since. You can still find him there, talking to empty snake skins.

Most adult birds lose their feathers (molt) once or twice a year. How are old feathers replaced by new ones? New feathers form under the bird's skin. Each new feather, sealed in a protective sheath, helps push the old one from its socket. The new feather then continues growing until it is full size. Just how many feathers do birds have? It depends. A hummingbird has the fewest, about 1,000. Most songbirds have between 1,200 and 4,600 feathers. Water birds have the most, with the emperor penguin topping the list with 30,000 feathers!

Out With the Old

A bird's outer feathers get a lot of wear and tear. As they get worn they need to be replaced. The process of replacing old feathers with new ones is called molting. (Molting, unfortunately, has nothing to do with staying young, as the tale implies.)

In most birds, only a few feathers are replaced at a time, so that the bird is always well-covered and able to fly. Molting time varies: Some perching birds take as little as five weeks, others as many as twelve. Ducks and other water birds molt a little differently. They shed and replace all their feathers at one time. This takes two to four weeks, during which time the birds stay hidden in a protected spot.

During a molt, you are likely to find feathers on the ground. This is a good time to start a feather collection. (For more on feathers, see pages 15, 19, 20 and 45.)

Wayfinders

Holawaka's journey between the sky kingdom and earth must have been a long one! Many backyard birds also regularly make long journeys. About half of the world's species divide their time between breeding ranges and wintering ones (or summer and winter homes). The yearly movement of birds between these two places is called migration.

Just how birds manage to get from one place to another—without the benefit of roads, maps, or compasses—has long intrigued humans. It seems birds get information about general direction from the sun (during the day), the stars (at night), and magnetic north (thanks to tiny crystals of magnetite situated above a bird's nostrils).

You can use some of these same means to help you find your way.

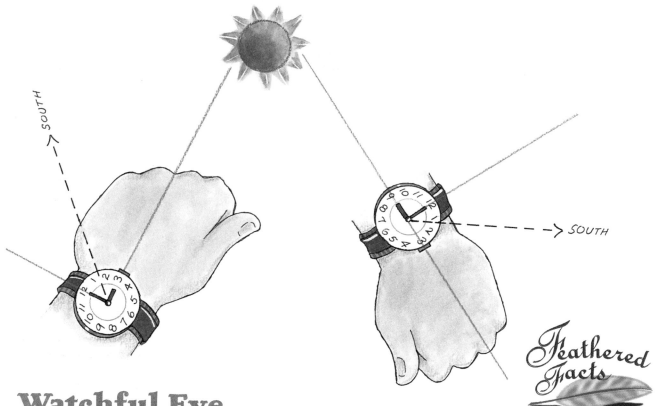

Watchful Eye

On a sunny day, you can find south with a watch (the kind with hands). Position yourself so that the hour hand points at the sun. Halfway between 12 and the hour hand is roughly south. (If it's before noon, that point is on the opposite side of your watch.) Note: During daylight savings time, use the point halfway between 1 and the hour hand.

Feathered Facts

Birds aren't the only animals that migrate. Certain fish, amphibians, insects, and mammals follow seasonal migrations. Many humans do, too. Do you know anyone who goes south to Florida, Arizona, or Mexico for the winter?

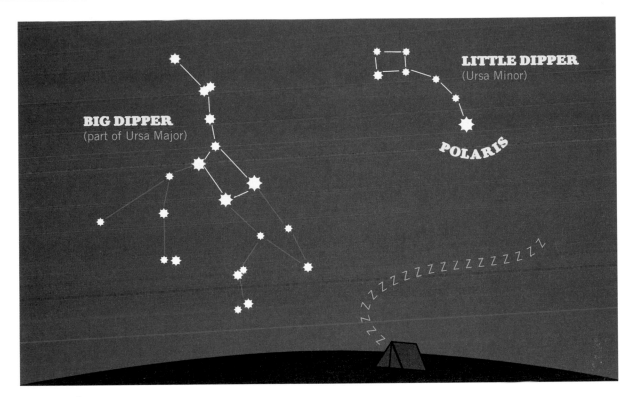

BIG DIPPER
(part of Ursa Major)

LITTLE DIPPER
(Ursa Minor)

POLARIS

Seeing Stars

At night, it's easy to find north. First, locate the Big Dipper. Trace an imaginary line from the top outermost star of its bowl to the last star on the handle end of the Little Dipper. That star is Polaris, also called the North Star. When you are facing Polaris, you are facing north.

Feathered Facts

Some birds don't have far to go when they head south for the winter; some species in the Rocky Mountains just move down the mountain a mile or so. Other birds have more daunting journeys. None is more impressive than the one made by the Arctic Tern. It travels the entire length of the globe— from one pole to the other—twice a year, a round-trip of more than 20,000 miles!

Arctic Tern

Feathered Facts

For centuries, no one knew where birds went when they migrated. Some people speculated they went into hibernation, joining frogs and turtles at the bottom of ponds. It was even suggested birds spent the winter on the moon. Talk about a long journey!

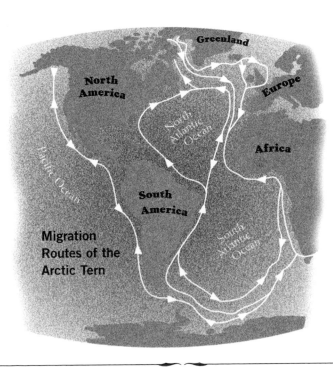

Migration Routes of the Arctic Tern

Greenland

North America

Europe

North Atlantic Ocean

Pacific Ocean

Africa

South America

South Atlantic Ocean

Who's Who

Holawaka never did properly identify the Galla people. Instead he mistakenly gave the secret of staying young to the wily snake.

You'll never mistake one bird species for another, thanks to this memory game you can make yourself. For hints on drawing birds, see the box on the next page.

1 Page through a bird identification guide, and choose ten to twenty birds to include in your deck. (You can always add more later.)

2 Draw detailed pictures of the birds on the index cards. Write the bird's common name beneath each picture. If you like, add the bird's Latin name plus additional information, such as a description of its call or the habitat in which it is found.

Remember, you need to create two cards of each bird.

REDHEADED WOODPECKER

To play the game, shuffle the cards and place them face down in rows. Taking turns, each player turns over any two cards, hoping to find matching cards. If a player makes a match, she picks up that pair and takes another turn. Play continues until all the pairs have been claimed. The player with the most matched pairs is the winner.

Feathered Facts

For added fun, illustrate the male of the species on one card and the female on the other. In some cases, the two look identical (black-capped chickadees, crows, and tree swallows all fit this description), but the males of many species have brighter feathers or other distinguishing marks.

Bald Eagle

Here's another idea: If you live in the United States, make a state bird deck. You'll only need 28 pairs of cards, since only 28 species are designated state birds. No less than seven states have chosen to honor the cardinal, while several other birds also appear on more than one state's list.

Quick Draw

Drawing birds is easy if you "build up" your pictures in layers.

First, visualize the bird as a series of simple shapes, such as circles, ovals, and triangles. Lightly sketch the shapes.

Turn the shapes into the various parts of the bird, adding more detail to your drawing, including any large areas of color. Carefully erase the shapes and any stray lines.

Last, color your drawing, adding shading to make the bird appear three-dimensional.

Weather...Or Not

There was a time when the average person was more aware of the natural world than most of us today. This included watching for signs of changing weather. Wind direction and the presence of certain clouds provided many clues. So did the behavior of animals, including that of birds.

Some of these clues were turned into catchy rhymes, making them easy to remember. People living by the sea invented this one:

> Sea gull, sea gull,
> Sit on the sand.
> It's a sign of rain
> When you're at hand.

Flocks of seabirds on land may very well mean a storm is on its way. Because air density drops before a rainstorm, birds find it harder to fly then and often wait until conditions improve.

Further inland, farmers once looked to barnyard birds for clues. When chickens rolled on the ground, rain was expected. Likewise:

> If a rooster crows when he goes to bed,
> He'll get up with rain on his head.

As you come to know the birds in your area, you may notice they act differently before a change in the weather. Can you predict the weather by their actions?

Role of Thunder

Many Native American peoples once believed the thunderbird was responsible for making thunder and bringing rain. Images of the eagle-like bird were drawn on everything from tepees to pottery.

Create a thunderbird design to decorate your belongings—from your school pack and notebooks to clothing. It's easy with a simple paper stencil and acrylic paint.

YOU NEED
- Freezer paper
- Craft knife
- Repositionable glue
- Acrylic paint
- Sponge

Note: Be sure to have an adult help you cut the stencil with the craft knife if you are not old enough to use one by yourself.

1 On the non-shiny side of a piece of freezer paper, draw a thunderbird design. Copy the Woodland Indian design shown, or come up with your own. (Note: The shiny side of the freezer paper will be face up when you stencil the design, reversing the image.)

2 Carefully cut out the stencil with the craft knife. Apply repositionable glue to the non-shiny side of the paper. Let dry according to package instructions.

3 Place the stencil, shiny side up, on the surface you wish to decorate. Dip a corner of a sponge into the paint, then dab at the open area of the stencil with the sponge. Carefully remove the stencil. Let the paint dry completely.

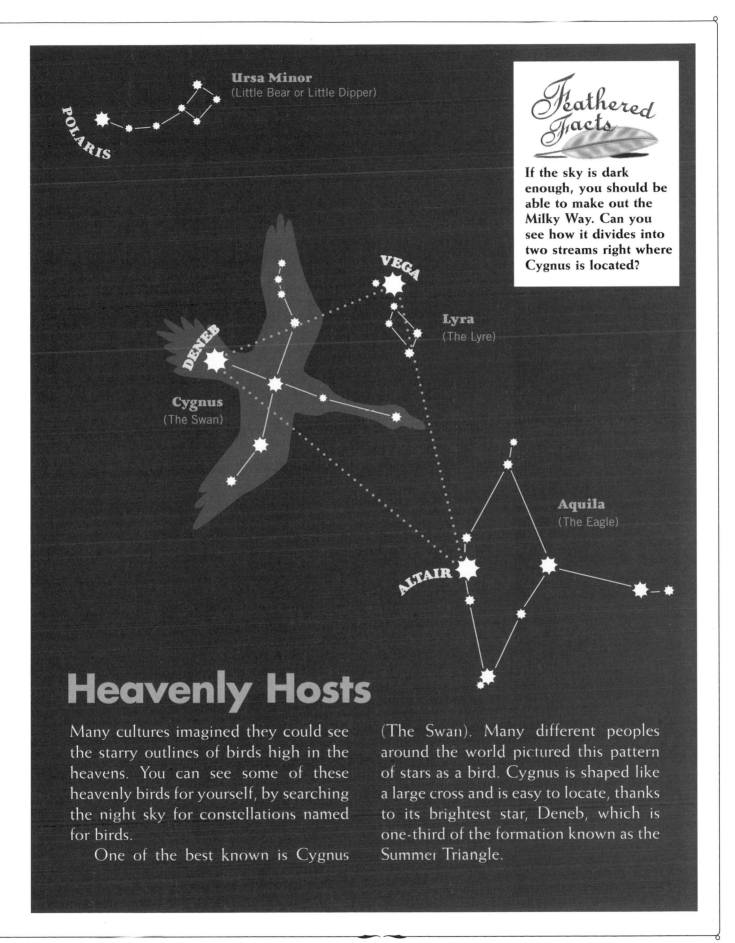

Ursa Minor
(Little Bear or Little Dipper)

POLARIS

VEGA

DENEB

Lyra
(The Lyre)

Cygnus
(The Swan)

Aquila
(The Eagle)

ALTAIR

Heavenly Hosts

Many cultures imagined they could see the starry outlines of birds high in the heavens. You can see some of these heavenly birds for yourself, by searching the night sky for constellations named for birds.

One of the best known is Cygnus (The Swan). Many different peoples around the world pictured this pattern of stars as a bird. Cygnus is shaped like a large cross and is easy to locate, thanks to its brightest star, Deneb, which is one-third of the formation known as the Summer Triangle.

The crane is much admired by the Japanese, who regard it as both a symbol of long life (the bird can live as many as 80 years in captivity) and of happy marriage (the birds choose a single mate for life).

The Gratitude of the Crane

The islands of Japan extend like a string of pearls in the azure sea. On the northernmost pearl—the island of Hokkaido—there once lived an old woodcutter and his wife.

Life was not easy for the old couple. Each day the man had to travel a little further from home to find enough firewood to sell, and each day his legs and back grew a little stiffer with age. Some days the woodcutter returned with only enough sticks to light the tiny stove in their home. Some days he returned with none at all.

On one such day during the grip of winter, the woodcutter was heading home empty-handed when he was startled to find a crane lying across his path. On closer inspection, the woodcutter saw that one of the bird's wings had been pierced by an arrow. Another man might have rejoiced at the discovery of such a promising meal, but the woodcutter's only thought was for the crane's comfort.

77

The Gratitude of the Crane

"Here now," said the woodcutter soothingly. "Just hold still, and I'll have that arrow out in no time." Slowly and carefully, all the while calming the bird with his talk, the woodcutter eased the arrow from the crane's wing. He wiped away the blood and cleansed the wound with a bit of water from his canteen. The bird rose to its feet, arched its graceful neck, and hesitantly flexed first one wing and then the other. Then, with a running start, the majestic creature leapt into the air and flew away.

During dinner that evening, the woodcutter told his wife about the wounded crane. "You did well to help the poor creature," she told him. "The crane is no ordinary bird. It should not be treated otherwise."

Just as the two were finishing their meal, there was a knock at the door. The woodcutter rose to answer it. A small girl, who appeared to be no more than ten years of age, stood there. Her clothes were tattered and torn, and much too thin to ward off the chill of the winter's night.

"Kind sir," the girl said, bowing deeply, "I have lost my way, and the night is cold. May I warm myself by your fire?"

The old man hurried the girl inside, seating her by the stove into which he threw some more sticks. His wife brought her a steaming bowl of miso soup. Clutching it for some time between her hands to warm them, the girl greedily drank it down.

"Child, why are you alone in the woods on such a night as this?" asked the old woman. "Where are your parents? Where is your home?"

"I have no parents," replied the girl. "At least none that I can remember. I was hoping to make it as far as the next village when I lost my way in the dark."

Never having been blessed with children, the woodcutter and his wife looked at one another and had the very same thought. "Then you must stay with us," they said. The girl thanked them and agreed to share their home.

Megumi (may-GOO-mee), as the young girl was called, had been favored with a disposition as sweet as plum wine. Each morning she awoke with a smile. She sang as she helped cook and clean the house; she skipped and pranced when she accompanied the woodcutter on his rounds. She was just as popular with the children her own age. She was eagerly sought out as a playmate by the boys and girls in the village, who laughed in delight when she danced for them, leaping into the air, her arms aflutter.

"Megumi has brought us such happiness," the woodcutter said to his wife one evening.

"Indeed she has, husband!" exclaimed the old woman. "I think often of the crane you saved in the woods that day. The gods must have seen fit to repay you in this way."

While the woodcutter and his wife never spoke of it, Megumi knew life was a constant struggle for them. One morning she said, "I know how hard it is to stock the larder and keep the house warm. Please allow me to help you. I am a skilled weaver. If I had a loom, I could weave a bolt of cloth that you could then sell."

The old man and his wife were reluctant to put the young girl to work in this way, but Megumi insisted and so the woodcutter built a loom for her. When it was done, the girl told the couple, "It will take seven days for me to weave the cloth. During that time, I must not be disturbed. Please do not worry about me, but please do not take even one peek at me while I am at my work." The old man and woman promised to honor Megumi's wishes.

Seven days later, when Megumi emerged from her room, the woodcutter and his wife were alarmed by the girl's appearance. Her face had no color and she was painfully thin. But their attention turned to the bolt of shimmering cloth that the girl held in her arms. It was unlike anything they had ever seen. The intricately woven pattern seemed to dance with life, yet the cloth was as light as a feather. It was most exquisite.

Megumi smiled and said, "This cloth should fetch a good price at the market. But do not set the price yourself. Let those who desire it offer what they think it is worth."

On market day, the woodcutter took the bolt of cloth to the village. He had hardly unwrapped it when a clothier stopped to stare at it, overwhelmed by the dazzling design.

"I'll give you one hundred gold pieces for this," the clothier said without hesitation. The woodcutter remembered what Megumi had said about letting others set the cloth's price. He was amazed to think that someone was offering one hundred gold pieces for it. His thoughts were interrupted by another bystander shouting, "I'll give you five hundred!"

"I'll double that!" declared a third. "This fabric is fit for the gods! I am the Emperor's tailor, and this cloth will make a splendid robe for His Royal Highness. Take my offer of one thousand gold pieces."

A murmur of excitement ran through the crowd of people that had gathered around the woodcutter. One thousand gold pieces! An unheard-of price for a bolt of cloth. But the Emperor's tailor was already counting out the coins, and so the woodcutter gave him the cloth in exchange for a bulging sack of gold.

Megumi only smiled knowingly when the woodcutter showed his wife the coins. "First you and now this," the two old people said, hugging the girl. "How can we ever thank you for the happiness you've brought us?"

"Dear ones, you have done much more than that for me," Megumi replied simply.

The three lived well for many years until there were only a few coins left in the money jar. "It is time I wove you some more fabric," announced Megumi one morning. "Please remember what I once told you. You must not disturb me while I am at my work, and you must not, under any circumstances, even glance at me while I am weaving." Once again, the old man and his wife agreed to Megumi's conditions.

Perhaps if the neighbors hadn't raised such doubts in their minds, the old couple would have found it easy to do as Megumi bid. But first one busybody and then another questioned why the old man and his wife should not watch the fabulous fabric taking shape. "Our daughters keep no secrets from us," they scoffed. "Besides, she's just weaving a piece of cloth. What harm can there be in watching her do it?"

"Megumi has asked us not to watch her, and we must abide by her wishes," the old woman explained. However, she had to admit that she did wonder what went on behind that closed door. She recalled how thin and pale Megumi had been after she'd woven the first bolt of cloth. And just how did the girl weave cloth without using thread of any sort?

Bird Tales from Near & Far

For six of the seven days, the old woman resisted the urge to spy on Megumi. But on the afternoon of the seventh day, she could hold back no longer. "Surely just a quick peek will do no harm," she thought to herself. "Megumi must be nearly done by now anyway." The old woman approached the door on tiptoe, and carefully opened it just a crack.

What she saw was truly shocking. There at the loom stood a blood-spattered crane, frantically pulling feathers from its own body and weaving them into cloth. The old woman suppressed a cry, then fainted and slumped to the ground.

When she came to, she saw that both her husband and Megumi were kneeling beside her. The girl held one of the woman's hands in her own, and reached for one of the woodcutter's before lowering her eyes. "I am so sorry that it had to end like this," she said, her voice barely above a whisper. "As you have already guessed, I am the crane whose life you saved so many years ago."

"I was allowed to become a human child, the one thing you had never had, so that I might repay the kindness you showed me. There was only one condition: If ever you were to discover my true identity, I would have to return to my previous form. I am afraid that I must go now, but I want you to know how much your love has meant to me, both when I was a bird and when I was a child."

Tears welled up in the woodcutter's eyes, and his wife began to sob quietly. "Come," Megumi said. "I wish to be with you until the very last." The girl gestured for the couple to follow her. They headed for a broad field. Once there, Megumi said, "Close your eyes, and count to seven before opening them. Good-bye, my beloved ones. I shall always remember you."

"And we shall never, ever forget you. Good-bye, crane-child," said the woodcutter and his wife, kissing the girl tenderly one last time. Then they

The Gratitude of the Crane

did as Megumi had asked, and when they opened their eyes they saw that the girl was no more. In her place stood a magnificent crane whose neck was proudly arched and whose feathers glistened like sunlit snow. The crane met their eyes, and held them in its gaze before bowing its head in mute acknowledgment. The woodcutter drew his wife to him as the crane bounded across the windswept field, gaining enough speed to send it aloft. They watched in silence as the bird rose into the sky, growing smaller and smaller as it was swallowed by the distance.

The Gratitude of the Crane

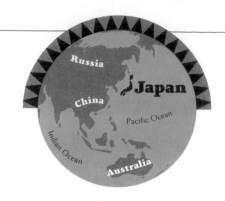

Russia

China

Japan

Pacific Ocean

Indian Ocean

Australia

The Word on Birds

The crane is by far the most beloved bird in Japan. There it has
been the inspiration for everything from decorative art to poetry.
This example of a short poem called a haiku manages to capture
the beauty and grace of cranes with only a few words.

> Cool seascape with cranes
>   Wading long-legged in the pools
>   Mid the Tideway dunes.

> —BASHO, 17TH-CENTURY POET

Like all haiku, this one is written on three lines, using a total
of only 17 syllables. (The first line has five syllables, the second
line seven, and the third line five.) Write your own haiku about
cranes, or about a bird that has special meaning for you. Can you
bring your bird to life with so few words?

Quick Quill

Make your haiku even more special by writing it with a pen made from—you guessed it!—a feather.

YOU NEED
- Large contour feather
- Craft knife
- Ink

Quill pens were once used extensively for writing in Europe, North America, and other parts of the world. They were usually made from the feathers of domesticated birds, such as geese and turkeys, although a large pen might be made from a swan feather.

You can make your own quill pen. Ask an adult to help you shape the quill if you are not old enough to use a knife by yourself.

1 Cut the quill at an angle, as shown.

2 Make two curved cuts, on either side.

3 Cut a small slit in the end, then trim the end at a slight angle. If you are right-handed, trim it at the slant shown. (Do the opposite, if you are left-handed.)

To write with the quill, first dip it in ink, wiping any excess onto the sides of the ink bottle. Press very gently on your paper. You'll need to dip the quill in ink quite often, perhaps every other letter or so. As the quill gets worn, snip off the end and recut the point.

Feathered Facts

Do you know how the penknife got its name? The small knife was originally used for cutting quills.

For more on feathers, see pages **15, 19, 20, 45 and 69.**

Warp and Weft

In the story, Megumi wove magnificent cloth from the feathers she pulled from her crane-body.

You can weave feathers and other items you find on nature walks—or at a special spot you visit each summer—into a keepsake tapestry. In this version, the loom you make from sticks also serves as the tapestry's frame.

1 Form a rectangle from four straight sticks. Lash the sticks together at each corner with short lengths of twine.

2 Wrap a continuous length of twine around two opposite sticks to make the warp, or the strings through which you will weave your found treasures. Tie securely.

3 Weave objects, such as feathers, decorative grasses, and wildflowers, in and out of the warp threads. Tie a hanging loop from the top crosspiece.

Feathered Facts

Woven fabric is made up of warp and weft. Warp is the name given to those threads arranged lengthwise on a loom. Weft refers to the threads woven across the warp to make the fabric.

Africa is home to several species of weaver-birds. The birds take their common name from the elaborate nests they weave from plant material. Some weaver-birds are communal nesters, with hundreds of birds all sharing a single tree.

Feathered Facts

Folktales featuring birds have provided the stories for several well-known ballets. "Swan Lake" is the work of Tchaikovsky, the Russian composer who lived from 1840 to 1893. Music for The "Firebird" was composed by fellow Russian, Igor Stravinsky (1882–1971).

Tales of bird-maidens (birds that turn into young girls or women) are found throughout the world. In Europe, the bird is usually a swan, although geese are commonly featured in Finnish tales. In Guyana, a small country on the coast of South America, the bird is usually a vulture.

Birds A-Leaping

It's no wonder that Megumi liked to dance. Cranes are among the finest dancers of the bird world. Males and females bow and leap when courting, but whole flocks of cranes have also been observed dancing rhythmically, apparently for the sheer joy of it.

Human dances based on the expressive movements of cranes are found in Japan, Africa, North America, and even Australia. Other birds dance, too, and several dances have been inspired by these. The Blackfoot Indians imitate the dance of the sage grouse; in Germany, a dance is patterned after that of a European grouse.

Invent your own dance movements based on bird behavior you have noted or seen on film. How might you show the scurrying movements of a sandpiper or the swoop of a swallow?

A Thousand Cranes

Origami, or paper folding, is a popular pastime in Japan. Not surprisingly, one of the best-loved origami models is the crane.

Although there are many steps to this model, it is not difficult to make. Take your time and make your folds as accurately as possible, creasing the paper well after each step.

YOU NEED
- Square sheet of light-weight paper, at least 6" (15 cm) in size

1 With the colored side up, fold the paper in half diagonally first one way and then the other. Unfold.

2 Turn the paper over, and fold the paper in half to make a rectangle, first one way and then the other. Don't unfold this last fold.

3 Holding the paper as shown, push your hands together to make the shape pictured.

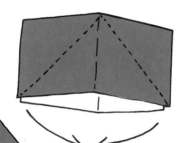

4 Fold the lower front edges in so that they meet at the center crease.

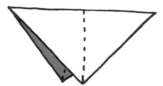

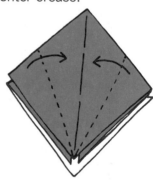

5 Fold down the top triangle.

6 Lift the triangle and unfold the folds you made in step 4. Lift the top layer of paper upwards, pulling it so the outer edges come together.

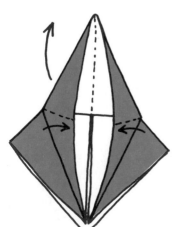

7 Flatten the diamond shape.

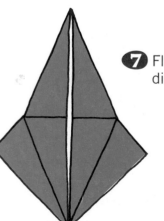

8 Turn the paper over and repeat steps 4 through 7.

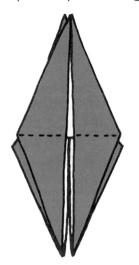

9 Fold the lower front edges in toward the center.

10 Turn the paper over, and repeat step 9.

11 Reverse fold the two lower portions. Reverse fold one of these to make the crane's beak.

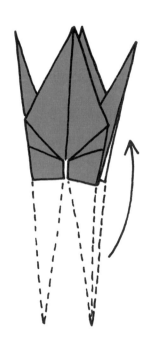

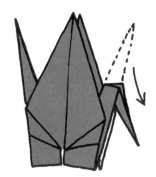

12 Pull the wings apart, which will cause the center triangle to flatten into a rounded hump.

TO REVERSE FOLD:
Fold the paper in half toward you; unfold, then fold away from you along the same crease line. Unfold completely. Push down, reversing the direction of the fold, as shown.

Feathered Facts

Folding paper cranes has been a popular Japanese activity for centuries, but after World War II, the models came to have a special significance.

It all started with a twelve-year-old girl named Sadako Sasaki, whose parents were killed by the atomic bomb the United States dropped on Hiroshima on August 6, 1945. Stricken by radiation sickness, Sadako began folding cranes from the pieces of paper that held her medicine. She hoped to fold one thousand cranes, believing that if she succeeded, she and the other children in the hospital would get well. Although she grew weaker daily, she continued folding paper cranes, but instead of hoping for her own recovery, she prayed for world peace. She had completed 644 cranes when she died.

When the children of Japan learned of Sadako's story, they carried on her work. Word spread, and soon people all over the world were folding cranes to join those Sadako had made. Thus the crane came also to symbolize world peace.

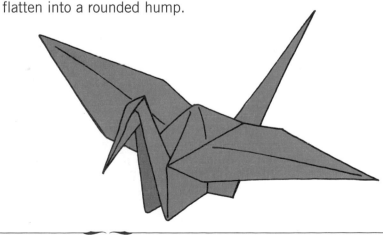

The Gratitude of the Crane

About the Tales

The stories in this book are just a few of the many tales featuring birds that are told around the world. All have been passed down from generation to generation, changing a little here and a little there along the way. In retelling these tales, I have taken bits and pieces from many sources. In short, I have done what all storytellers do: made these retellings my own. I hope you enjoyed reading them and that you'll carry on the tradition, altering them as you see fit and passing them along to other listeners.

Why Owl Hides During the Day

The Iroquois of the eastern United States and Canada tell many tales that serve to explain the characteristics or behavior of animals. The last line of this story hints at the purported wisdom of owls. Why are owls thought to be such wise birds? It may be because an owl's face resembles a human one, thanks to its large, unblinking eyes set close together in the front of its face. (Not that humans always act wisely, of course!)

Mark My Words

This tale from Thailand is a blend of fact and fiction. While many parrots are capable of mimicking human speech (even, some researchers insist, communicating intelligently with humans in a limited way), lorikeets are not among them. In many countries throughout the world, members of the parrot family—talkers and non-talkers alike—are kept as pets.

The Palace of Beaks

The hoopoe, the hero of this tale found throughout the Middle East, is often associated with Solomon, the king who ruled ancient Israel nearly three thousand years ago. While the bird is a handsome creature, especially when its crest is fully fanned, its nesting habits leave much to be desired. Made in the cavities of trees, hoopoe nests are remarkably filthy and foul-smelling.

The Farmer and the Tsar of the Crows

While owls are thought to be wise birds, crows (and closely related ravens, magpies, and jays) are, in fact, the most intelligent of our avian friends. Many studies have been made of their social structure, varied methods of communication, and amazing ability to learn. The crows in this story are probably hooded crows, a species found throughout a broad area of Europe.

The Messenger Bird

Much African lore includes heavenly messengers whose job is to deliver important information to the people on earth. In some versions of this Galla tale from Ethiopia, Holawaka gives the secret of immortality to the snake in exchange for part of a mouse the reptile is eating. As punishment, the bird is not only banished to earth but condemned to eat carrion, or the flesh of dead animals, forevermore.

The Gratitude of the Crane

This favorite Japanese tale has several different well-known versions. In one, the woodcutter is a young man who lives alone in a cottage in the forest. The crane he rescues is transformed into a young woman, who later becomes his wife. Like the child in the story in this book, the woman turns back into a crane when the secret of her magnificent weaving is revealed. This tale has also been the subject of a play and an opera in Japan.

Index
To Activity Sections

More Good Children's Books From
WILLIAMSON PUBLISHING

Kids Can! Books from Susan Milord

ADVENTURES IN ART *(Newly revised)*
Arts & Crafts for 8- to 13-Year-Olds
  by Susan Milord
160 pages, 10 x 8 ½, Trade paper, $12.95

DR. TOY BEST VACATION PRODUCT AWARD
THE KIDS' NATURE BOOK *(Newly revised)*
365 Indoor/Outdoor Activities and Experiences
  by Susan Milord
160 pages, 10 x 8 ½, Trade paper, $12.95

HANDS AROUND THE WORLD
365 Creative Ways to Build Cultural Awareness &
Global Respect
  by Susan Milord
160 pages, 10 x 8 ½, Trade paper, $12.95

Tales Alive! Books from Susan Milord

BENJAMIN FRANKLIN BEST JUVENILE/YA FICTION AWARD
PARENTS' CHOICE HONOR AWARD
SKIPPING STONES MULTICULTURAL HONOR AWARD
TALES ALIVE!
Ten Multicultural Folktales with Activities
  by Susan Milord
128 pages, 8 ½ x 11, Trade paper, $15.95

TALES ALIVE!
Bird Tales From Near & Far
  by Susan Milord
96 pages, 8 ½ x 11, Trade paper, $14.95

BENJAMIN FRANKLIN BEST MULTICULTURAL AWARD
BENJAMIN FRANKLIN BEST JUVENILE/YA FICTION AWARD
PARENTS' CHOICE APPROVED
LEARNING™ MAGAZINE TEACHERS' CHOICE AWARD
TALES OF THE SHIMMERING SKY
Ten Global Folktales with Activities
  by Susan Milord
128 pages, 8 ½ x 11, Trade paper, $15.95

Kaleidoscope Kids™ Books

MEXICO!
50 Activities to Experience Mexico
Past & Present
  by Susan Milord
96 pages, 10 x 10, Trade paper, $10.95

AMERICAN BOOKSELLER PICK OF THE LISTS
DR. TOY BEST 100 CHILDREN'S PRODUCTS AWARD
CHILDREN'S BOOK COUNCIL 1998 NOTABLE CHILDREN'S
  TRADE BOOK IN THE FIELD OF SOCIAL STUDIES
PYRAMIDS!
50 Hands-On Activities to Experience Ancient
Egypt
  by Avery Hart and Paul Mantell
96 pages, 10 x 10, Trade paper, $10.95

KNIGHTS & CASTLES
50 Hands-On Activities to Experience the
Middle Ages
  by Avery Hart and Paul Mantell
96 pages, 10 x 10, Trade paper, $10.95

To see what's new at Williamson and learn more about specific books, visit our website at: http://www.williamsonbooks.com

TO ORDER BOOKS:

You'll find Williamson books at your favorite bookstore or order directly from Williamson Publishing.
We accept Visa and MasterCard *(please include the number and expiration date)*, or send check to:

WILLIAMSON PUBLISHING COMPANY
CHURCH HILL ROAD, P.O. BOX 185
CHARLOTTE, VERMONT 05445

Toll-free phone orders with credit cards:
  1-800-234-8791

E-mail orders with credit cards:
  order@williamsonbooks.com

Catalog request: mail, phone, or E-mail

Please add **$3.00** for postage for one book plus
50 cents for each additional book. Satisfaction
is guaranteed or full refund without questions
or quibbles.

Prices may be slightly higher when purchased
in Canada.

Kids Can!®, *Little Hands*®, and *Tales Alive!*®, are registered trademarks of Williamson Publishing. *Kaleidoscope Kids*™ is a trademark of Williamson Publishing.